Spotlight on Reading

Inferring
Grades 3–4

Frank Schaffer

An imprint of Carson-Dellosa Publishing LLC
Greensboro, North Carolina

Credits

Layout and Cover Design: Van Harris

Development House: The Research Masters

Cover Photo: © Getty Images

 This book has been correlated to state, common core state, national, and Canadian provincial standards. Visit *www.carsondellosa.com* to search for and view its correlations to your standards.

Frank Schaffer

An imprint of Carson-Dellosa Publishing LLC

PO Box 35665

Greensboro, NC 27425 USA

www.carsondellosa.com

ISBN 978-16-099-6490-0

05-133137784

About the Book

The activities in *Inferring* are designed to improve students' reading comprehension. The skill of inferring, using information to draw logical conclusions, is a higher-level thinking skill—a difficult one for young students to master. Inferring requires the reader to make educated guesses based on prior knowledge and on information that is implied but not directly stated. In this book, articles, poems, and cartoon strips are supplemented with a variety of activities to make learning the skill of inferring fun! The exercises increase in difficulty as the book progresses, so the students practice more advanced skills as they work through the activities.

With a variety of formats, teachers can provide direct instruction, reinforcement, or independent practice throughout the year. Have students work with partners or teams to complete the more challenging activities.

Table of Contents

A Pea Wee Plea

Read the poem. Use context clues to infer the answers to the questions.

I cannot tell how long I'll last.

My appetite is shrinking fast!

Dad said I had to eat these peas

Despite my constant, begging pleas.

This vegetable is shaped so odd!

Why should food come in a pod?

Dad, please do not be mean,

Don't make me eat anything green!

1. Why does the girl think that peas are a strange vegetable? _____

    _____

2. What is the girl hoping her dad will do? _____

    _____

3. How do you think Dad will react to his daughter's request? _____

    _____

Name _____

Read the poem. Use context clues to infer the answers to the questions.
Circle the answers.

Come and see our awful school play—
I have to be a turtle today.
Tommy's a bear, and Jill's a fox.
Their costumes are comfy—mine's a box.
Marty's a bobcat, and Mike's a dog,
Luis gets to be a colorful frog!
Turtles bite: all animals beware!
Just kidding! This snapping turtle won't
     scare!

1. How does the boy feel about his part in the play?

    He likes it.   He does not like it.

2. Which words describe the boy's feelings and opinions about his costume?

    uncool   embarrassing   jealous

    fun   uncomfortable   pretty

3. Which words describe his feelings and opinions about his classmates'
    costumes?

    uncool   embarrassing   jealous

    fun   uncomfortable   pretty

Excuses, Excuses!

Read the poem. Use context clues to infer the answers to the questions.

My dog chewed it before I got to class!
I hope my teacher will give me a pass.
The teacher says, "No, my story is not right,"
But Mom threw the paper out last night.
The teacher says, "No, that cannot be true,
Why didn't you finish the work that was due?"
I've got more excuses to put to the test,
But telling the truth is probably best.

1. What is the speaker referring to? _____

   _____

2. Do you think the teacher believed the speaker? _____

3. What do you think happens next? _____

   _____

   How do you know? _____

   _____

An "Eggciting" Discovery

Read the poem. Use context clues to infer the answers to the questions.

• •

I discovered an egg in my yard.

Its shell is large and very hard.

I know it must be very old,

It's surrounded by a lot of mold.

When my reptile hatches, I'll be so proud!

Its baby cry will be so loud.

We'll go walking, it will look distinct,

Towering above me—it's NOT extinct!

1. What kind of animal does the speaker think will hatch out of the egg?

   _____

2. Name three clues that helped you guess its identity.

   a. _____

   b. _____

   c. _____

3. If you found this egg, do you think it would hatch? _____

   Why or why not? _____

   _____

7

Name _____

Read the poem. Use context clues to infer the answers to the questions.
Circle the answers.

"Rake those leaves and bag them
   all,
Or there will be no basketball!"
Mom sure knows how to ruin a day
And I was all geared up to play.
I know just what I'll do instead—
I'll pretend those leaves are my own
   bed.
I'll lie down underneath that pile,
Stay very still, and wait awhile.
I've changed the game 'cuz I'm unique.
I love playing Hide-and-Seek!

1.   What was the speaker determined to do today?

   do chores   call his friends   play basketball

2.   Describe how the speaker's mom will react to his game of "Hide-and-Seek."

   She will laugh.   She will be unhappy.   She will join the game.

3.   What game do you think mom will want the speaker to play next?

   "Hopscotch"

   "Rake the Leaves and Bag Them Quick"

   "Baseball"

Name_____

Read the poem. Use context clues to infer the answers to the questions.

I need to go across the street,
But it's hard to walk on eight sore feet.
Can I climb upon this person's shoe?
I'll rest and get home fast, too!
Wait a minute! My home's back there,
I can't see my web anywhere.
. . . One hour later, and miles away . . .
Just my luck to ride a jogger today.

1. Who is the speaker? _____

2. What clues tell the speaker's identity? _____

    _____

    _____

Can We Trade?

Read the poem. Use context clues to infer the answers to the questions. Circle the correct answers.

Tony's lunch looks tastier than mine!
He must know the way to dine.
He traded with me; I was ready to eat.
But the best looking food belonged to Pete!

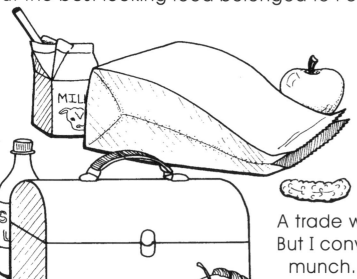

A trade was hard, Pete wanted his lunch,
But I convinced him to switch; I was ready to munch.
When I tasted his food, it wasn't that great.
But Tony and Pete both cleaned their plates!

1. The speaker was judging the other lunches by their . . .

    a. taste.   b. smell.   c. appearance.

2. How do you know that Tony and Pete were satisfied with their new lunches?

    a. They were willing to trade.

    b. They cleaned their plates.

    c. Their food looked good.

3. Did the speaker like his new lunch?

       yes   no

    How do you know? _____

Inferring • CD-104554

Read Between the Lines

Look at the comic and read the story. Use context clues to infer the answers to the questions. Circle the correct answers.

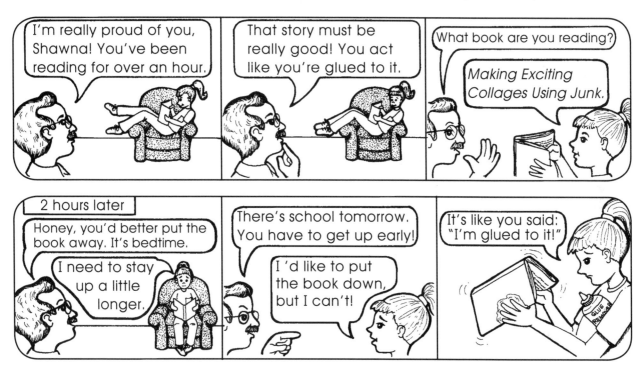

1. You think that . . .
   a. Shawna really enjoys reading.
   b. The book is not very interesting.
   c. Shawna will not make collages again.

2. While Dad thought Shawna was reading, she was probably . . .
   a. trying to get her hands off the book.
   b. talking on the telephone.
   c. creating collages.

3. When you are "glued" to a book, it means you are . . .
   a. repairing the book.
   b. examining the book.
   c. really interested in the book.

Try This: What do you think happened next? Draw your idea on a separate piece of paper.

11

Horsin' Around

Look at the comic and read the story. Use context clues to infer the answers to the questions. Circle the correct answers.

1. You can tell that Jimmy wants to . . .
   a. be a cowboy when he grows up.
   b. roughhouse with his dog.
   c. make a huge mess.

2. "Mosey" means to . . .
   a. travel slowly or to stroll.
   b. look.
   c. jump.

3. Jimmy's mom thought Jimmy . . .
   a. was playing an exciting game.
   b. chose a game that should not be played indoors.
   c. was very creative.

4. Buck . . .
   a. loves pretending to be a horse.
   b. thinks that Jimmy is a good cowboy.
   c. does not like Jimmy's idea of horseplay.

Idioms

Read the story. Use your inferring skills and context clues to answer the questions below.

• •

1. Sydney sent out twelve invitations for her summer vacation party. She was making a reservation at a local pool, so she needed to know how many of her friends were coming. At the bottom of each invitation she wrote **RSVP** and her phone number.

   RSVP means:

   Please come.   Please do not come.   Please reply.

2. Andrew's father gave him an allowance. He used it to buy all the little things he wanted when they went to the mall. Usually, he received one dollar each week. One week, his father got a bonus at work. He gave Andrew five dollars.
   "Will I get five dollars every week?" Andrew asked.
   "No," his father said. "Just **once in a blue moon**."

   Once in a blue moon means:

   Once a month   When the moon is blue   Not often

3. Ethan's father lost his job. His mother went back to work, but her job does not pay very well. Ethan had to help out. Instead of eating in the school cafeteria, Ethan made sandwiches to take to school. It was fun. It was also his way to help the family **make ends meet**.

   Make ends meet means:

   Have enough money   Find a job   Tie a rope

The Mysterious Message

Read the story. Use context clues to infer the answers to the questions on the next page.

• •

Junior Detective Jonathan Wilson held a mirror in one hand and a Morse code book in the other. He was trying to figure out how to reflect sunlight with the mirror. He wanted to flash messages to his friend Miguel who lives in the house across the street. He and Miguel got the idea from a spy movie on television.

Jonathan glanced over at Miguel's window. Something flashed. There were long flashes and short flashes. It was a message! Jonathan wrote down a dash for each long flash. He wrote down a dot for each short flash. When the flashing stopped, he looked at his code book and translated the dots and dashes to letters. The message said, "C-o-m-e q-u-i-c-k."

Jonathan climbed down the ladder. He wondered why Miguel wanted him to come. The two of them did most of their detective club business up in the tree. It was more secret.

When he knocked on the door to Miguel's room, his friend asked for the password. It took Jonathan a minute to remember it. "Operation Reflect," he said.

The door opened. "It took you long enough," Miguel said.

Blake, another boy in their class, was sitting on Miguel's bed. Jonathan waved to him and made himself comfortable in the chair by Miguel's window.

"So what's going on?" Jonathan asked.

"Blake has a case for us," Miguel said. "It's a secret message. He found it when he came home from school."

Miguel handed Jonathan a white pillow case. The message was printed on the fabric in pale blue. It was a group of strange symbols.

"What does it mean?" Blake asked.

"We've been trying to figure it out for an hour," Miguel said.

Jonathan spread the pillowcase out on his lap. He happened to look up and see his reflection in the mirror on Miguel's closet door.

"I know!" Jonathan said. He held the pillowcase up to the mirror. Miguel and Blake laughed.

"Somebody must have dropped some junk mail in the laundry," Blake said.

Friday Only: Two Pounds for the Price of One.

Hold this page up to a mirror. What does the message say?

The Mysterious Message (cont.)

Circle the correct answers. You may have to circle more than one answer.

• •

1. What kind of clubhouse did Jonathan and Miguel have?

    a cave   a tree house   a shed

2. What symbols are used in Morse code?

    dots and dashes   red and blue   long and short

3. What does each group of Morse code symbols stand for?

    a secret place   a person   a letter of the
                                                       alphabet

4. The word **reflection** comes from which word?

    fleck   reveal   reflect

5. What must have happened while Blake was at school?

    His mom washed his pillowcase.

    His mom went shopping.

    His mom walked the dog.

6. What kind of sale was the advertisement in the secret message about?

    clothes   shoes   groceries

Telephone Chatter

Read the story. Use context clues to infer the answers to the questions. Circle the correct answers.

· ·

"Hi, Jacob. This is Lamar. Do you want to come over and play outside?"

"Sounds great! What do you want to do?"

"I love playing in this weather. I thought it might be fun to build a snowman."

"That would be cool! Let's make a really big one and dress him up like our favorite sports player! I'll bring a jersey, a helmet, and some huge shoulder pads."

"I can get my dad's spiked shoes and a ball. Dress warm! I just heard the weather forecast."

"Let's both call a couple of friends and meet in your front yard in fifteen minutes."

"Okay. Bye!"

1. The boys' snowman will look like a . . .
   a. golfer.
   b. football player.
   c. baseball player.
2. It's appropriate for this snowman to be big because . . .
   a. these athletes are usually big.
   b. all snowmen should be big.
   c. Jacob only likes to build big snowmen.
3. The weather is probably . . .
   a. wet and humid.
   b. sunny and pleasant.
   c. very cold and snowy.

4. Lamar . . .
   a. enjoys winter activities.
   b. gets cold easily.
   c. prefers playing indoors.
5. Jacob . . .
   a. only likes to follow his own suggestions.
   b. enjoys playing with others.
   c. prefers the summer.

Misty's Morning Out

Read the story. Use context clues to infer the answers to the questions. Write the answers below.

• •

Misty lived in a beautiful cage in the middle of Rosa's bedroom. Misty's favorite spot in her lovely home was her cardboard tunnel. It smelled of raw oats—one of Misty's favorite treats.

On cage-cleaning day, Rosa would take Misty's cage into the backyard for a good cleaning. She put Misty in a little exercise pen while her home was being cleaned. The world outside smelled different— fresh and green.

One morning, while Rosa was cleaning Misty's cage, Misty saw a butterfly. At first, Misty was scared. She thumped her back feet in warning. The pretty butterfly continued to flutter above her, and Misty wanted a closer look. She gave a big hop and found herself outside the little pen. The cool grass tickled her feet. She gave a little hop, then another.

A loud, shrill sound from the sky made Misty's long ears stand on end. Misty caught sight of a large bird flying towards her very fast. She ran. She saw an old metal bucket turned on its side

near the fence. Misty dashed inside the bucket. The bird gave a shriek of disgust and flew into a large tree. Misty did not move. She stayed in the bucket a long while, just to be safe, and fell asleep.

She awoke to the sound of Rosa calling her name. Misty hopped out of her hiding place. The day was warm, and the sun was at the top of the sky. She stood on her back legs and sniffed the air. All of a sudden, she found herself in Rosa's arms. Rosa held Misty tightly against her face. Rosa's cheeks were wet. "Strange," thought Misty. "It is not raining."

Rosa took Misty inside to her bedroom. Misty's cage, clean and shiny, sat on the table. There was a dish of raw oats and a carrot waiting just inside the door. A new cardboard tunnel made from an oatmeal container awaited her. Misty wriggled her nose. She had enough adventure for one day. She was glad to be home.

1. What kind of animal was Misty? _____

   How do you know? _____

2. About what time did Misty wake up in the bucket? _____

   How do you know? _____

Frog Facts

Read the story. Use your inferring skills and context clues to answer the questions on the next page.

• •

Did you know there are more than 3,000 types of frogs in the world? They are all **fascinating**.

A lot of frogs do not use their hands to help them eat. They use their tongues instead! Frogs roll out their long, sticky tongues and snare insects, snails, and spiders. Using the muscles in their tongues, they gulp down the snack.

Swallowing food can be hard. Frogs use their eyes to help push the food down to their stomachs! Those bulging eyes can sink down to help force dinner down a frog's throat.

Frogs have lungs, but they do not breathe in all of their air. Some of the air comes into their bodies through their skin! Water can enter a frog's body through its skin, too. Frogs must keep their skin damp for it to be healthy. When it is hot and dry, some frogs burrow underground where it is cool and moist. Others stay in the mud by streams and ponds.

Like lizards and snakes, frogs shed their old skins to **reveal** new ones. The frog pulls his old skin off over his head. Then he eats it! Frogs can shed once a week.

Different kinds of frogs have different talents. Some are good diggers. Many can swim and hop. Some frogs can jump twenty times their own length. The Costa Rican flying tree frog sails from one branch to another! It uses its webbed feet like parachutes.

Frogs are amphibians. That means they live two-part lives. Baby frogs, called tadpoles, are water animals. They change, or **metamorphose**, into adult frogs that are land animals.

Some kinds of frogs are **endangered**, so there are not many of their kind left. In fact, some environmental researchers consider them pests. Bullfrogs are **ferocious** eaters. They can **devour** all other animals in a pond! Bullfrogs are not endangered, though.

Frog Facts (cont.)

Circle the meaning of the words in **bold**.

• •

1. The word **fascinating** means:

    important   interesting   ordinary

2. The word **reveal** means:

    to eat veal again   to uncover   to cover up again

3. The word **metamorphose** means:

    to change   to meet someone   to eat food

4. The word **endangered** means:

    taking over an area, such as a pond

    very hungry

    in danger of disappearing from nature

5. The word **devour** means:

    to eat   to sleep   to grow

6. The word **ferocious** means:

    gentle   fierce   tired

Camping Out

Read the letter. Use context clues to infer the answers to the questions. Circle the correct answers.

• •

Dear Grandma and Grandpa,

　　We are camping at Bear Forest. All sorts of interesting things have happened. Freddy ran off with one of the stakes for the tent and buried it somewhere. That's okay, though. A lopsided tent has lots of character. Today, we went hiking in the forest for most of the day. I collected some really interesting plants that have leaves that grow in clumps of three. I wanted to show you some, but Mom told me to get rid of them right away. After supper, we built a big bonfire and got marshmallows out to toast, but a sudden thunderstorm forced us into our tent. (That's why I'm writing you this letter.) The rain is fine with me. Worms are crawling around everywhere, and Dad says they will come in handy tomorrow.
　　I guess that's all for now. Besides, I can't seem to stop itching!

　　　　　　　　　　　　　Love,
　　　　　　　　　　　　　Mikey

1. Freddy . . .
    a. likes to play tricks.
    b. is Mikey's neighbor.
    c. is the family dog.

2. Mikey . . .
    a. loves to write letters.
    b. looks for the bright side of situations.
    c. is angry about the trip.

3. Mom . . .
    a. really likes to go camping.
    b. realized the plant was poisonous.
    c. does not like collecting plants and flowers.

4. Tomorrow, Dad . . .
    a. is planning to go fishing.
    b. wants to repair the tent.
    c. hopes to move to another campsite.

Name _____

Abracadabra

Look at the picture and read the story. Use context clues to infer the answers to the questions. Circle the correct answers.

• •

Leo liked to pretend he was a magician. He knew magic was not real, but it was fun to create illusions. He practiced with Gerardo, his pet rabbit. The two imagined Leo could pull a carrot out of Gerardo's ear.

1. In Leo's imagination, both he and Gerardo. . .

    enjoy doing magic tricks together more than anything else.

    are thinking about food.

    have practiced for many years.

2. If the two magicians always do similar tricks at the same time, what do you think the rabbit would do if the boy magician pulled a coin out from behind a friend's ear?

    hop around   pull a leaf from behind his ear   pull out another carrot

3. Circle the word that describes Leo.

    tricky   outgoing   imaginative   clever

4. What other things do you think Leo likes imagining?

    illusions with mirrors   science experiments   card games like Go Fish

Name _____

Being Prepared

Look at the comic and read the story. Use context clues to infer the answers to the questions. Circle the correct answers.

1. You can tell that . . .
   a. the girls can swim well.
   b. swimming can be a lot of fun.
   c. the girls are very excited.

   How do you know? _____

   _____

   _____

2. Another word that means
   "**definitely**" is . . .
   a. absolutely.
   b. hardly.
   c. maybe.

3. You believe that . . .
   a. the girls are sisters.
   b. the girls have gone snorkeling before.
   c. the girls will call other friends to join them.

   What clue words in the story tell you the answer? _____

   _____

4. The girls will probably . . .
   a. dive to the bottom of the pool.
   b. take off some items before swimming.
   c. go home for dinner.

   How do you know? _____

   _____

Outer Space

Look at the comic and read the story. Use context clues to infer the answers to the questions. Circle the correct answers.

Shane and Tia loved watching stars. They could study the stars that they learned about in science class. They could imagine aliens watching them too!

1. You can tell that both kids . . .

    a. have excellent eyesight.

    b. like science.

    c. have bad imaginations.

2. You know that the time is some-time . . .

    a. between 12 P.M.–3 P.M.

    b. between 3 P.M.–6 P.M.

    c. after 8 P.M.

3. Both Shane and Tia . . .

    a. tend to exaggerate their bravery.

    b. are very brave.

    c. examine all facts before jumping to conclusions.

4. The creatures in the tree are . . .

    a. two little, green Martians.

    b. two raccoons.

    c. four screech owls.

Picnic Mystery

Read the story. Use context clues to infer the answers to the questions on the next page.

• •

My friend Francine has a very vivid imagination. Her explanations for the most common events can be very colorful.

Last month, Francine's family and my family went on a picnic to the park. We played games, ran races, and eventually sat down to eat. First, we emptied my mom's picnic basket. She had packed hot dogs, buns, strawberry fruit bars (my favorite), and pretzels. Then we began to empty the basket that Francine's mom had packed. Out came some egg salad sandwiches, potato salad, cold juice, and . . . !

"What happened to the potato chips?" exclaimed Mrs. Farmer. "There was a full bag of them when I packed the basket!"

"I bet I know what happened, Mom," Francine began to explain. "The ants at this park are horrendous! They must have chewed their way into the bag and carried away some of the chips!" You know how strong those little creatures are!" she continued, looking very serious. "I noticed some of them when Becky and I were climbing the hill. I'm sorry I didn't say something."

"That sounds a little far-fetched," replied Mrs. Farmer, "but maybe that could have happened. We'll discuss this matter further when we get home."

We sat down at the picnic table. I thought I heard some crunching noises when Francine plopped down on the bench. However, I may have been imagining it. Anyway, lunch was great—minus some of the chips!

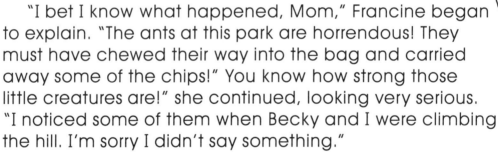

Picnic Mystery (cont.)

1. Do you think Francine's explanation for the missing potato chips was accurate? _____ Explain. _____

   _____

2. Did Mrs. Farmer totally accept Francine's explanation? _____
   How do you know? _____

3. Explain this statement: "Her explanations for the most common events can be very colorful." _____

   _____

4. What could have caused the crunching noises that were heard when Francine plopped down? _____

   _____

5. Underline each correct statement.

   Realistically, you can guess that . . .

   • Becky has heard Francine's wild explanations before.

   • Francine actually saw ants carrying off the potato chips.

   • Becky is Francine's friend.

   • Mrs. Farmer always believes her daughter.

   • Francine had probably eaten the chips sometime earlier.

6. Circle all the words that best describe Francine's explanation for the missing potato chips.

   honest   sincere   mischievous   crafty

         imaginative   creative   kind

Bear Scare

Read the story. Use context clues to infer the answers to the questions. Write the correct answers.

• •

Ebony and her brothers, Darius and Forrest, sat around the campfire. The flames cast an eerie glow on Forrest's face as he told his story about a lost camper and a bear.

The campfire crackled. Ebony shivered as red-gold embers floated skyward.

Forrest grinned. "Are you scared?" he asked.

Ebony shook her head. "No, I'm just cold."

"I'll get a blanket from the tent," Darius said as he scampered off into the dark.

"Don't finish the story until Darius comes back," Ebony said.

"Are you sure you aren't scared?" Forrest asked.

Ebony felt something fuzzy land on her head. "GRRRRRRRR!" Ebony jumped. Her head smacked into her brother's nose.

"Ow!" Darius yelled.

"I'm sorry," Ebony said. She was shaking. "You surprised me!"

Darius rubbed his nose and laughed. "I guess I deserved it."

"Should I finish the story?" asked Forrest.

"No!" said Ebony.

Darius smiled at the worried look on his sister's face. "Let's tell jokes instead."

1. At what time of day did this story occur? _____

    What are the clues? _____

    _____

2. What landed on Ebony's head? _____

    How do you know? _____

    _____

3. Was Ebony afraid? _____

    How do you know? _____

    _____

Name _____

 Presents!

Read the letters. Use context clues to infer the answers to the questions.
Circle the correct answers.

• •

Dear Kenny,

   I really enjoyed talking with you on the phone. I remembered how you said you enjoy "catching flies." I was a little surprised, but I guess everyone has a special hobby.

   Anyway, I got this for you as a special present. I hope you like it!

               Love,
               Aunt Tillie

Dear Aunt Tillie,

   Thank you so much for the bug catcher. I enjoy using it and find it can be very challenging. I was very surprised! I'm used to catching baseballs, but I guess there are all sorts of ways to catch flies!

               Love,
               Kenny

1. Kenny . . .

    a. did not express himself clearly to his aunt.

    b. collects flies and all sorts of bugs for a collection he's had for years.

    c. told Aunt Tillie exactly what he wanted for birthday present.

2. Aunt Tillie . . .

    a. knew precisely what Kenny enjoyed doing.

    b. was wrong about Kenny's hobby.

3. Kenny really wanted . . .

    a. a fly swatter.

    b. a baseball mitt.

    c. flypaper.

Building Houses

Read the story. Use context clues to infer the answers to the questions on the next page. Circle the correct answers.

• •

Wolfsburg Gazette

February 6, 2011

Tests of Building Materials

Our star reporter tested the quality of three housing materials. The results were shocking!

Straw was the weakest. Wind forces of only 10 mph left a small straw house in disarray. "I wouldn't live in this type of house," the reporter said.

Next he tested houses made of wooden sticks. Strong wind forces of 30 mph caused a stick dwelling to fall over. "Sticks may be popular with dogs, but they should not be used to build houses," the reporter said.

His final experiment tested bricks. "I found bricks to be sturdy. My many attempts to knock over the walls failed," the reporter said.

Please note: This assignment left our reporter a little winded. He will not be on assignment again until next month.

Building Houses (cont.)

1. Why did the reporter not want to live in a straw house?

   A. He does not like straw.

   B. It is not safe.

   C. He does not like wind.

2. "Disarray" means . . .

   A. very neatly arranged.

   B. somewhat messy.

   C. totally disorganized.

3. Which type of house would the reporter recommend?

   A. Straw

   B. Stick

   C. Brick

4. What would be the most likely name of the reporter?

   A. Larry Lamb   B. Wolf Blitzen   C. Percival Pony

Big Dreams

Read the story. Use context clues to infer the answers to questions on the next page.

When I grow up, I am going to build a huge store where boys and girls can find any toy they want. There will be one room filled with dolls that can walk, run, skate, talk, eat, smile, and even read a book with you!

Another room will have cars and trucks that you can drive (after fastening your seat belt, of course). Game boards will be so huge that you can become a living piece that moves. How many games do you play now where the pieces walk to the next square?

If you like puzzles, you can play in my puzzle room. Three-dimensional puzzles can be put together and pulled apart.

Another room will be the size of a soccer field. Here you will be able to bounce, throw, and hit balls without having to hear your parents say, "You have to play outside!"

The best thing about my store would be that it never closes. You could stay as long as you wanted! Also, you would not have to pay for anything!

No adults would be allowed in the store—not even parents! I would make the door so tiny that only kids would be able to enter.

I guess I have thought of everything, except . . . Oops! There could be one big problem!

Name _____

1. What is the problem that the speaker is thinking about at the end of the

   story? _____

   _____

   _____

2. How can you tell that the speaker is "safety conscious"? _____

   _____

   _____

3. Circle the words that describe how the speaker feels as he tells of his big
   plans.

   content   motivated   tranquil   relaxed   excited

4. Is the speaker very realistic? _____ Why or why not? _____

   _____

5. Do you think the store will be smaller than a soccer field, the size of a

   soccer field, or larger than a soccer field? _____

   How do you know? _____

   _____

Lost in Space

Look at the comic and read the story. Use context clues to infer the answers to the questions. Circle the correct answers.

The astronauts were headed to a new planet, but they made a wrong turn. They had to stop at a space station to ask for directions. They were not sure where they stopped, but there were some clues. They were on a large red planet, and the aliens called themselves Martians.

1. On what planet did the astronauts stop?

   Venus   Mars   Saturn

   How do you know? _____

   _____

   _____

2. To which planet did the astronauts want to go?

   Venus   Mars   Saturn

   How do you know? _____

   _____

   _____

Time Travelers

Look at the comic and read the story. Use context clues to infer the answers to the questions. Circle the correct answers.

Paige and her brother Reid loved learning about history. They wanted to travel to the past. Paige thought she could see how the pyramids were built. Reid wanted to discover how Columbus sailed the ocean blue.

1. You can tell that . . .
    a. the time machine is very advanced.
    b. Paige and Reid want to travel to the future.
    c. Paige and Reid know lots of history.

2. Another word for **product** is . . .
    a. machine.
    b. result.
    c. cube.

3. If Paige and Reid traveled ahead in time, they might see . . .
    a. Pilgrims settling in America.
    b. Abraham Lincoln being declared president of the U.S.
    c. people saluting a U.S. flag with 51 stars.

4. To create their time machine, it took Paige and Reid . . .
    a. less than an hour.
    b. about an hour.
    c. more than an hour.

Name _____

Keisha and Malia like giving advice. They write a column in the newspaper. Read their advice column. Use context clues to infer the answers to the questions on the next page. Circle the correct answers.

• •

The Princely Press

Amazing Advice from the Star Stepsisters

January 21, 2011

Dear Keisha and Malia,

My mom keeps nagging me to clean my room! I think it looks great. Besides, I do not want to give up any of my prized possessions. Do you have any suggestions?

Pig Pen

Dear Pig Pen,

There is a very simple solution to your problem. Just answer the question: "Why do you think beds are built so high off the floor?"

Keisha

. . . May I add that good housekeepers are very hard to find. Some just want to party, party, party!

Malia

Dear Keisha and Malia,

I have been invited to a special party, and I don't know what to wear. I know that the two of you have attended fancy balls. Can you give me some of the latest fashion ideas?

Plain Jane

Dear Jane,

You have come to the right place for advice! Clothing design is one of our specialties. Dots, dots, and more dots. Wear polka dots of every color and size. Then everyone will "spot" you the moment you make your grand entrance!

Malia

. . .Don't forget that your hair needs to be noticed, too! I suggest attaching lots of feathers so that it will appear soft and fluffy. May I suggest small, downy feathers for the front and large plumes for the back? Don't forget to duck under low entrances!

Keisha

. . . Oh, Sister dear, you "quack" me up!

Malia

Dear Sisters (cont.)

1. How would you describe Pig Pen?
   a. He enjoys having a clean room.
   b. He has very expensive toys and possessions.
   c. He does not mind having a messy room.
   How do you know? _____

   _____

2. How would you describe Keisha and Malia?
   a. They prefer shortcut solutions to problems.
   b. They give very responsible and sound advice.
   c. They are very serious people.
   How do you know? _____

   _____

3. If Plain Jane followed the stepsisters' advice, what would probably happen at the party?
   a. Everyone would be jealous of Plain Jane.
   b. People would not like Jane's outfit.
   c. Plain Jane would be admired.

4. What word describes Keisha and Malia?

   timid   nasty   peculiar   funny   envious

   How do you know? _____

   _____

5. Would Pig Pen's mom be satisfied with the stepsisters' advice?

   yes   no

   Why or why not? _____

   _____

35

Name _____

Hannah's Promise

Read the story. Use context clues to infer the answers to the questions. Circle the correct answers.

• •

C-D-E-F-G. Hannah pounded out the notes on the keys. As she warmed up her fingers, she glanced at the clock. "Two minutes." Hannah groaned. When she begged her mother for music lessons last August, she promised she would practice thirty minutes every day.

Hannah sighed, opened her music book, and began to play the song with the title circled in ink. She did not play for long. She wiggled on the bench and glanced out the window. Her friend Tasha was jumping rope. Hannah looked at the clock and groaned. "Five minutes."

Hannah played until she reached a hard part. Her fingers always tangled and tripped on the black and white keys. The sour notes made Hannah cringe. Her eyes wandered to the calendar on the wall. Saturday was circled in red—only three more days. Would she be ready?

Hannah attacked the difficult passage. She played it over and over until her fingers hit every note.

Was the clock even working? The hands moved so slowly! Hannah played the piece from the beginning. To her surprise, she played it all the way through with no mistakes. Hannah smiled. Can I do it again?" she asked herself.

She tried, and she did! She played the piece two more times with no mistakes. "I could play this with my eyes closed!" Hannah giggled.

Her mother walked in the room. "You have been practicing for 45 minutes. You may go outside and play," she said.

"In a minute, Mom. Just one more time," Hannah said with a grin. Saturday was going to be a great day.

1. What instrument does Hannah play?

    violin   trombone   piano   drums

2. What do you think will happen on Saturday?

    a jump rope competition   a music recital   a baseball game

3. When she started, did Hannah want to practice?

    yes   no

    How do you know? _____

_____

Name _____

Read the letters. Use context clues to infer the answers to the questions. Circle the correct answers.

• •

April 2, 2011

Dear Omeka,

How is everything in New York? It's been just over a week, but I really miss you! Do you remember how we always talked about getting a pet? Well, here in Texas, I am finally able to have one. Wags is so much fun! He wags his tail every time he sees me. He curls up into a ball when he sleeps. He even plays fetch. You would think he was a dog! The only difference is, he does not bark. His meows are very loud though.

I can't wait for you to visit and meet Wags!

Your best friend,
Rachel

April 8, 2011

Dear Rachel,

It was great receiving your letter. Wags sounds really cool! During the summer, I hope to get acquainted with him. I just got a new pet, too! Fluffy is so cute. She has the softest fur and such a bushy tail. I just love her long ears. I have so much fun watching her run and play. For now she sleeps in a little shoebox. When I visit you, I won't bring Fluffy. She hops away too easily. She might get lost on a Texas farm!

Write soon!

Love,
Omeka

1. Rachel has been gone for . . .

    a. 1–7 days.   b. 8–14 days.   c. 15–21 days.

2. Wags is a . . .

    a. rabbit   b. dog   c. cat

3. Fluffy is a

    a. rabbit   b. dog   c. cat

Tyler on the Mound

Read the story. Use context clues to infer the answers to the questions on the next page.

• •

Tyler's stomach lurched as he opened the car door. He clutched his mitt and pulled on his ball cap. He looked anxiously at the diamond-shaped field where his teammates gathered. Tyler was the new pitcher for the Hawks. Braden, their former pitcher, moved away last week, and Coach asked Tyler to take his place on a trial basis. "Good grief!" Tyler said. "I'm the pitcher."

Tyler joined his teammates on the field for warm-ups and stretches. His eyes wandered to the area where their opponents, the Tigers, stretched and moved like large jungle cats. The Tigers were giants, and they had big muscles. They had to be a lot older than he was, Tyler was sure of it.

"What's wrong?" asked Jake, Tyler's best friend. "You look like you ate my sister's Eggplant Surprise. The surprise was she forgot to take it out of the oven when the timer buzzed. Yuck."

Tyler did not laugh at his friend's joke. "I haven't pitched before, not in a game!" he said. "If I make a mistake, we could lose!"

Jake scratched his head. "Same thing was true when you played right field. It didn't stop you from playing."

"I guess," Tyler said.

Tyler took his place on the pitcher's mound. Harsh stadium lights blocked out the stars, and the crowd roared in the stands. Even though the air was cool, sweat stung his eyes. He looked into the stands and saw his parents smile. He looked at the coach, and the coach gave him a serious nod, the sign to start the game. He looked at the boy at bat, and the boy glared back at him.

Tyler looked at Jake, who crouched behind home plate.

Jake gave Tyler a wide, goofy grin. "Come on, Ty! You can do it! Put it here." he yelled, holding his mitt as a target.

Tyler took a deep breath, wound up, and pitched. Swish! The batter swung and missed. Jake tossed the ball back to Tyler, and Tyler let the second pitch fly even faster. The batter swung so hard he spun around, but he didn't hit the ball, Tyler burned a third pitch directly across the plate. Whump! The ball struck Jake's mitt, and the umpire yelled, "You're out!" The batter scowled, dropped the bat, and returned to the dugout.

The next batter for the Tigers was even bigger than the first. He scowled at Tyler, but Tyler just smiled. His heart beat in a slow, steady rhythm as he focused his attention towards the plate.

Tyler on the Mound (cont.)

Write the answers to the questions.

• •

1. What game did Tyler play? _____

   How do you know? _____

   _____

2. What time of day was it? _____

   How do you know? _____

   _____

3. How did Tyler feel about pitching at first? _____

   How do you know? _____

   _____

4. What was Tyler's biggest worry about pitching? _____

   How do you know? _____

   _____

5. How did Tyler feel about pitching at the end of the story? _____

   _____

   How do you know? _____

   _____

6. What position does Jake play? _____

   How do you know? _____

   _____

Gardening with Garth

Read the article. Use context clues to infer the answers to the questions on the next page.

- -

The Midwest Advance

March 6, 2011

Do you like beans? Lots of beans? If so, this report will knock your socks off! While traveling through the Midwest, I met the world's best bean expert. His name is Jack, and he loves to grow bean plants. He especially loves growing lima beans, navy beans, kidney beans, and soybeans.

His plants are enormous. Most are so tall they must be tied to poles to stay up. Jack's plants appear to vanish among the clouds!

Jack has a lot of advice for farmers. He stresses that bean plants should be planted in rich, loose, warm soil. However, he refuses to share his special secret for such unbelievable plant growth.

As Jack's success becomes known around the country, many people will want to travel to see the beans. I advise travelers not to come by plane. The local airport is closed because of blockages in the sky. These blocks may or may not be related to the plants. However, it is well worth your time to find a different way to travel and visit!

For my next article, I am off to view a pumpkin patch. It is rumored that these pumpkins grow so big people actually live in them!

-Garth

Gardening with Garth

Circle all the correct answers.

. . . .

1. Why will Jack not share his secret for plant growth?

    All small bean plants would die.

    Other farmers would try to grow similar bean plants.

    Large bean plants would fill the skies.

    People would stop eating beans.

2. Which of the following means of transportation would Garth suggest you use to visit Jack?

    a. car   b. jet   c. helicopter   d. bus

    How do you know? _____

    _____

    _____

3. Jack's plants . . .

    are probably very strong.

    are probably taller than Jack's house.

    probably produce large beans.

    are similar to other bean plants.

    How do you know? _____

    _____

    _____

41

A Light in the Garden

Read the story. Use clues in the story to infer what really happened. Answer the questions on the next page.

• •

Hugo sat in the chair by the window. The grandfather clock by the stairs started to chime. It echoed through the quiet halls.

Hugo could hardly keep his eyes open. He knew his pajamas were laid out neatly on the bed, but he did not want to put them on. Tonight, he wanted to sleep in his clothes, not in the flannel pajamas with blue footballs all over them.

When his parents said he could stay with his uncle while they went to France, Hugo had been happy. His other choice was Camp Blue Sky. He hated Camp Blue Sky. At least at his uncle's house, he would have good food, a room of his own, and no camp crafts.

However, tonight Hugo was missing his parents.

Hugo closed his eyes and listened to the clock strike. He wished he had chosen Camp Blue Sky. At least there were other people around.

The clock stopped chiming. The huge house was very still. His uncle's bedroom was far down the hall. Hugo opened his eyes and looked out the window. He wanted to see something moving. If he knew for sure somebody else, was nearby he might be able to sleep. Other people made him forget that Mom and Dad were far away.

At first, he saw nothing, just dark paths and the reflection of the moon in his uncle's pond. Then he saw it. At first, the white beam flickered. It became steady. It moved across the far side of the garden, just beyond the garage. When it came toward the house, Hugo no longer felt alone. But who was it? What was it?

He jumped in bed. He did not want anybody to see he had been missing his parents. His heart pounded. He heard the creaking boards. They sounded like footsteps. His bedroom door creaked open. "Who could it be?" Just then something soft and warm touched him. A wet tongue washed his face.

"Hugo, it's only me!" His uncle pulled a flashlight from his pocket and turned it on so he could see. "I brought Felix in out of the cold. He needs a place to sleep. Would it be ok for him to sleep in here? He always likes company."

Hugo laughed. "Yes. that would be great!"

A Light in the Garden (cont.)

Inferring will help you answer these questions. Write the correct answers.

1. What made the creaks that Hugo heard? _____

   _____

   _____

2. What made Hugo not want to go to bed? _____

   _____

   _____

3. Who really wanted company? _____

   _____

   _____

4. Why did Hugo's uncle really come to Hugo's room? _____

   _____

   _____

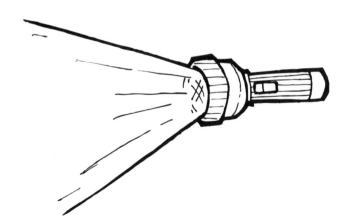

43

Emily's Sheltie

Read the story. Use context clues to infer the meaning of words in bold. Answer the questions on the next page.

• •

Emily wanted a dog. Her mother and father were not sure. They did not think Emily would take care of a pet. Emily begged and begged. Finally, her mother stopped **resisting**.

"Emily," her mother said. "You can have a dog, but you have to **select** a breed that is suitable for our **urban** home." She told Emily that books and magazines might suggest appropriate dogs.

Emily thought her mother was trying to **discourage** her, but she was not going to give up. She went to the library every day. She found out how to train a dog. She found out how to **modify** annoying behavior, such as raiding trashcans. She learned how to **encourage** a dog to obey commands. She even found out how to **prevent** common diseases, so her pet would not get sick!

Emily also looked at pictures. She saw beagles, Irish wolfhounds, Chihuahuas, German shepherds, poodles, and huskies. All of the breeds looked fun, but they were not right for her.

Then she saw a picture of a sheltie. She knew that was the kind of dog she wanted. The sheltie looked like a small collie, with fluffy fur and dark eyes. She learned that sheltie was short for Shetland sheepdog. Shelties help shepherds take care of sheep.

Emily showed the sheltie to her mother. Her mother thought it was a very nice breed of dog. Together, they researched where to adopt a sheltie puppy. They found an animal rescue organization near their house.

They visited the rescue group, and Emily got to hold a puppy. The minute she held a sheltie in her arms, she knew she had made the right choice.

Emily's Sheltie (cont.)

Circle the meaning of the words in **bold**.

• •

1. Emily had to **select** a calm dog.

   train   choose   receive

2. Emily had to find a **suitable** breed.

   fitting the situation   not too large   very intelligent

3. She learned how to **modify** bad habits.

   keep   change   repeat

4. They had an **urban** home with a small yard and many neighbors.

   city   country   mountain

5. Annoying **behavior**, such as barking, could be a problem.

   treat   appointment   habit

6. She knew how to **train** her dog not to bark.

   teach   ride   trip

7. She wanted to **encourage** her dog to do the right thing.

   punish   blame   convince

8. She did not want her pet to catch a **disease**.

   ball   illness   Frisbee

Answer Key

Page 4
Answers vary. Examples:
1. They are green; 2. let her not eat peas; 3. He will make her eat peas.

Page 5
Circle: 1. He does not like it. 2. uncool, embarrassing, uncomfortable; 3. fun, pretty, jealous.

Page 6
Answers vary. Examples:
1. homework; 2. no; 3. The speaker tells the truth. The speaker says telling the truth is best.

Page 7
Answers vary. Examples:
1. a dinosaur; 2. a. egg is old; b. poem talks about reptiles; c. speaker imagines the animal is not extinct; 3. No, because the egg is moldy.

Page 8
Circle: 1. play basketball; 2. She will be unhappy. 3. "Rake the Leaves and Bag Them Quick."

Page 9
Answers vary. Examples:
1. a spider; 2. eight feet; home is a web.

Page 10
Circle: 1. C; 2. B; 3. no.
Write: 3. Because the poem says it wasn't that great. (Written answers vary.)

Page 11
Circle: 1. A; 2. A; 3. C.

Page 12
Circle: 1. A; 2. A; 3. B; 4. C.

Page 13
Circle: 1. Please reply; 2. Not often; 3. Have enough money.

Pages 14–15
Circle: 1. a tree house; 2. dots and dashes, long and short; 3. a letter of the alphabet; 4. reflect; 5. his mom washed his pillowcase; 6. groceries.

Page 16
Circle: 1. B; 2. A; 3. C; 4. A; 5. B

Page 17
Answers vary. Examples:
1. a rabbit. Because she likes carrots and hops. 2. noon. Because the sun was high.

Pages 18–19
Circle: 1. interesting; 2. to uncover; 3. to change; 4. in danger of disappearing from nature; 5. to eat; 6. fierce.

Page 20
Circle: 1. C; 2. B; 3. B; 4. A

Page 21

Circle: 1. are thinking about food; 2. pull a leaf from behind his ear; 3. imaginative; 4. illusions with mirrors.

Page 22

Circle: 1. C; 2. A; 3. B; 4. B
Write: 1. They can't wait to get in the water. 3. snorkeling again. 4. There is not enough room in the pool with all of the items. (Written answers vary.)

Page 23

Circle: 1. B; 2. C; 3. A; 4. C.

Pages 24–25

Answers vary. Examples:
1. No. It seems unbelievable. 2. No. She said it did not seem right. 3. It means she makes up wild stories. 4. Potato chips in Francine's pocket. 5. Underlined: Becky has heard Francine's wild explanations before; Francine had probably eaten the chips sometime earlier. 6. Circled: mischievous, imaginative; creative

Page 26

1. At night. They needed a fire to see. 2. A blanket. Darius left to get a blanket and he was behind Ebony when it landed on her head. 3. Yes. She was shaking. Answers will vary.

Page 27

Circle: 1. A; 2. B; 3. B

Page 28–29

Circle: 1. B; 2. C; 3. C; 4. B

Page 30–31

Answers vary. Examples:
1. He cannot have a store just for kids if he is an adult! 2. He made sure kids wore seat belts in his toy cars. 3. Circle: motivated, excited. 4. No. He cannot have a store without adults. 5. Larger than a soccer field; because he said one room was the size of a soccer field.

Page 32

Circle: 1. Mars; 2. Saturn
Written answers will vary but may include : 1. There are Martians. 2. The astronaut asks how close they are to Saturn.

Page 33

Circle: 1. C; 2. B; 3. C; 4. B

Pages 34–35

Circle: 1. C; 2. A; 3. B; 4. peculiar, funny; 5. no; Written answers vary but examples are: 1. He does not want to clean his room. 2. They do not give good advice. 4. Their answers are odd and not very helpful. 5. The sisters tell him a shortcut to cleaning, which means his room will not really be clean.

Page 36

Circle: 1. piano; 2. a music recital; 3. no; Write: 3. She was groaning. (Written answers vary.)

Page 37

Circle: 1. B; 2. C; 3. A.

Pages 38–39

Answers vary. Examples:
1. Baseball. He wore a mitt and was a pitcher. 2. Night. The field lights were on, and they blocked the stars.
3. Nervous. His stomach twisted.
4. The team would lose. He told his friend. 5. Confident. He smiled.
6. Catcher. Jake told him to put the ball in his mitt, the target. He was also crouched behind the plate.

Pages 40–41

Circle: 1. Other farmers would try to grow similar bean plants. Large bean plants would fill the skies.
2. Car, bus. 3. Are probably taller than Jack's house, probably produce large beans. Write: 2. Garth said not to fly. 3. They touch the sky and are very large. They need support poles. (Written answers vary.)

Pages 42–43

Answers vary. Examples:
1. His uncle coming to his room.
2. Hugo missed his parents. 3. Hugo.
4. His uncle came to help Hugo not feel lonely.

Pages 44–45

Circle: 1. choose; 2. fitting the situation; 3. change; 4. city; 5. habit; 6. teach; 7. convince; 8. illness